IN MEMORY OF ISRAEL GOLLANCZ

John Milton's

EPITAPHIUM DAMONIS

Printed from the First Edition

With a new translation

by

WALTER W. SKEAT

(e Coll. Christ.)

CAMBRIDGE

AT THE UNIVERSITY PRESS

1933

CAMBRIDGE UNIVERSITY PRESS
Cambridge, New York, Melbourne, Madrid, Cape Town,
Singapore, São Paulo, Delhi, Mexico City

Cambridge University Press
The Edinburgh Building, Cambridge CB2 8RU, UK

Published in the United States of America by Cambridge University Press, New York

www.cambridge.org
Information on this title: www.cambridge.org/9781107673816

© Cambridge University Press 1933

This publication is in copyright. Subject to statutory exception
and to the provisions of relevant collective licensing agreements,
no reproduction of any part may take place without the written
permission of Cambridge University Press.

First published 1933
Re-issued 2013

A catalogue record for this publication is available from the British Library

ISBN 978-1-107-67381-6 Paperback

Cambridge University Press has no responsibility for the persistence or
accuracy of URLs for external or third-party internet websites referred to in
this publication, and does not guarantee that any content on such websites is,
or will remain, accurate or appropriate.

T HIS translation of Milton's commemoration of
his friend Charles Diodati was made as a tribute
to Sir Israel Gollancz by one of his oldest friends,
son of the late Professor W. W. Skeat, his chief teacher
at Cambridge. In the belief that the tribute is one with
which Sir Israel would have been especially pleased, the
friends who formed a committee to honour his memory
have caused it to be printed, primarily for distribution
to the subscribers to the memorial.

The Latin text printed above it is taken from an
anonymous and undated edition of the poem in pam-
phlet form of which the single copy known was pur-
chased by the British Museum in 1857, but has only
recently been entered in the General Catalogue under
Milton's name. It appears to be the editio princeps,
printed for private circulation. Its text is here exactly
reproduced save for the correction, noted in the mar-
gins, of five obvious misprints and the expansion of
a contraction.

A. W. POLLARD

EPITAPHIVM DAMONIS.

ARGVMENTVM

Thyrsis, & Damon eiusdem viciniæ pastores, eadem studia sequuti a pueritiâ amici erant, ut qui plurimùm. Thyrsis animi causâ profectus peregre de obitu Damonis nuncium accepit. Domum postea reversus, & rem ita esse comperto, se, suamque solitudinem hoc carmine deplorat. Damonis autem sub personá hîc intelligitur Carolus Deodatus ex urbe Hetruriæ Luca paterno genere oriundus*, cætera Anglus, ingenio, doctrina, clarissimisque cæteris virtutibus, dum viveret, iuvenis egregius.

* Ed. Princeps onundus

Thyrsis and Damon, shepherds of the same neighbourhood, had followed the same pursuits, and had been friends from childhood of the closer sort. Thyrsis, who had gone abroad for the cultivation of his mind, heard the news of Damon's death while in foreign parts. Afterward, returning home, and having discovered it to be as stated, he laments his own solitariness in this ode. Now the character of Damon is here meant for Charles Deodati, sprung on his father's side from Lucca, a city of Tuscany; in all other respects, an Englishman, whose intellect, learning and his other most shining virtues, showed him to have been, in his lifetime, a youth pre-eminent.

DAMON.

HIMERIDES nymphæ (nam vos & Daphnin & Hylan
Et plorata diu meministis fata Bionis)
Dicite Sicelicum Thamesina per oppida carmen
Quas miser effudit voces, quæ murmura Thyrsis,
Et quibus assiduis exercuit antra querelis
Fluminaque fontesque vagos, nemorumque recessus
Dum sibi præreptum queritur Damona, neque altam
Luctibus exemit noctem loca sola pererrans.
Et jam bis viridi surgebat culmus arista,
Et totidem flavas numerabant horrea messes,
Ex quo summa dies tulerat Damona sub umbras
Nec dum aderat Thyrsis, pastorem scilicet illum
Dulcis amor Musae Thusca retinebat in urbe.
Ast ubi mens expleta domum, pecorisque relicti

ATTEND, ye Nymphs who are of Himera's well,
For in your memories, yet, doth Daphnis dwell—
And Hylas, yet too ye remembering mourn
Dead Bion's many days lamented urn—
By citied Thames sing a Sicilian air!
Sing Thyrsis' words pour'd forth with heavy cheer,
Each murmur low, and moan'd uncessant tear—
Plaints that he search'd withal each cavern'd nook,
Each grove retir'd, river and wandering brook
Sorrowing for Damon reft him—nor would spare
Deep night his griefs, wandering o'er regions bare.
Twice with green ear the rising haulm 'gan swell,
Their harvests twice the golden granges tell,
  Since that last Dawn
Unto the Shades below had Damon drawn—
Nor yet was Thyrsis come; true, him o'erlong
In Tuscan city held soft charm of song!
But when a mind full furnish't, and the thought
Of his abandon'd flock him homeward brought,

Cura vocat, simul assuetâ sedítque sub ulmo,
Tum vero amissum tum denique sentit amicum,
Cæpit & immensum sic exonerare dolorem.
    Ite domum impasti, domino iam non vacat, agni.
Hei mihi quæ terris, quæ dicam numina cælo?
Postquam te immiti rapuerunt funere Damon!
Siccine nos linquis, tua sic sine nomine virtus
Ibit, & obscuris numero sociabitur umbris?
At non ille, animas virgâ qui dividit aureâ
Ista velit, dignumque tui te ducat in agmen
Ignavumque procul pecus arceat omne silentum.
    Ite domum impasti, domino iam non vacat, agni.
Quicquid erit, certè nisi mè lupus antè videbit*,
Indeplorato non comminuere sepulchro,

* Ed. Pr. has a
full-stop here.

And soon as 'neath the accustom'd elm he sate,
He then (then at last smote full his comrade's fate)
Thus gan to unload his measureless sorrow's weight!
    Home, lambs, unfed; no time for you have I!

Oh, how could I bespeak, as deities,
The powers that dwell on earth or in the skies,
Now that their harsh precept thy life hath rent?
Canst quit me so? Shall thy clear spirit be fled
Unsung, to fellow all the obscure Dead?
So may not Hermes make arbitrement,
But may He with His golden sceptre-head
    That doth the Souls divide—
Thee to a troop of thee judg'd worthy, guide,
Far from the herd of mute and stockish pent.
    Home, lambs, unfed; no time for you have I!

Yet be thou sure, so chance no wolf prevent
    My sight and strike me dumb,
    Whatever hap may come
Thou shalt not wholly moulder in the grave

7

Constabitque tuus tibi honos, longúmque vigebit
Inter pastores, illi tibi vota secundo
Solvere post Daphnin, post Daphnin dicere laudes
Gaudebunt, dum rura Pales, dum Faunus amabit:
Si quid id est, priscamque fidem coluisse, piúmque
Palladiásque artes, sociúmque habuisse canorum
    Ite domum impasti, domino jam non vacat, agni.

Hæc tibi certa manent, tibi erunt hæc præmia Damon,
At mihi quid tandem fiet modò? quis mihi fidus
Hærebit lateri comes ut tu sæpe solebas
Frigoribus duris, & per loca fæta pruinis,
Aut rapido sub sole, siti morientibus herbis

Unwept, but high establisht honour have
To thrive among our swains for many a day!
To thee (the next from Daphnis) cheerly they
   Their orisons will pay;
To thee (the next from Daphnis) will they raise
   Cheerly their songs of praise—
So long as in our country leas and lawns
Great Pales shall delight, delight the Fauns,—
If aught avail to have cherish'd gods of yore,
And what devout, and arts of Pallas' lore—
If aught avail to have had a Bard to friend.
   Home, lambs, unfed; no time for you have I!

Dead shepherd, thine this meed, these sureties too!
   But unto me what end
   Remains? what comrade true
Will cleave as thou, how closely, to my side?
Who will with me, as thou so oft, abide
Hard winter, and lands where the teem'd hoar-frost lies,
Or scalding noons, when parch'd the green herb dies?

Sive opus in magnos fuit eminùs ire leones
Aut avidos terrere lupos, prǽsepibus altis;
Quis fando sopire diem, cantuque solebit?
  Ite domum impasti, domino iam non vacat, agni.

Pectora cui credam? quis me lenire docebit
Mordaces curas, quis longam fallere noctem
Dulcibus alloquiis, grato cùm sibilat igni
Molle pyrum, & nucibus strepitat focus, at malus auster
Miscet cuncta foris, & desuper intonat ulmo
  Ite domum impasti, domino iam non vacat, agni.

Aut æstate, dies medio dum vertitur axe,
Cum Pan æsculeâ somnum capit abditus umbrâ
Et repetunt sub aquis sibi nota sedilia nymphæ,
Pastoresque latent, stertit sub sepe colonus,

  Who aid when I
Must lions huge, at range of spear, assay,
Or startle rav'ning wolves from sheepfolds high?
Who lull with speech, with song, the lingering day?
  Home, lambs, unfed; no time for you have I!

To whom now trust my heart?—Who'll teach me how
  To deaden eating care,
  Or with sweet converse low
The livelong watches of the night to snare,
When juicy pears hiss mid the genial glow
And crackle of chestnuts on the hearth resounds?
Without, the felon South with sky confounds
The earth, and on the elm his thunder sounds!
  Home, lambs, unfed; no time for you have I!

When summer days on noontide axle turn,
  When in the tall oaks' shade
Conceal'd, Great Pan himself to rest is laid;
When to their watery haunts the nymphs return;
When swains lie close; 'neath hedge the plowmen snore;

Quis mihi blanditiásque tuas, quis tum mihi risus
Cecropiosque sales referet, cultosque lepores?
  Ite domum impasti, domino iam non vacat, agni.

At iam solus agros, iam pascua solus oberro
Sicubi ramosæ densantur vallibus umbræ
Hic serum expecto, supra caput imber & Eurus
Triste sonant, fractæque agitata crepuscula silvæ.
  Ite domum impasti, domino iam non vacat, agni.

Heu! quàm culta mihi priùs arva procacibus herbis
Involvuntur, & ipsa situ seges alta fatiscit!
Innuba neglecto marcescit & uva racemo,
Nec myrteta juvant, ovium quoque tædet, at illæ
Mærent, inque suum convertunt ora magistrum
  Ite domum impasti, domino jam non vacat, agni.

Tityrus ad corylos vocat, Alphesibœus ad ornos,

Who shall thy graces lost to me restore,
—Laugh, polished wit, and salt of Cecrops' taste?
  Home, lambs, unfed; no time for you have I!

Companionless, o'er field—o'er farm I haste
Companionless, and now in bottom glade
Where'er thick branchings weave a deepening shade,
Wait dark! O'erhead, the gale moans with the showers;
Thro' shuddering dusk the stormwreckt forest lowers!
  Home, lambs, unfed; no time for you have I!

Woe's me! what wanton growths involve so fast
My once well-furrow'd fields! what mildew blast
Chokes my tall corn! on the unmarried vine
  The untended clusters pine,
Nor myrtles please, and irks the shepherd's hook;
The mournful flock up to their master look!
  Home, lambs, unfed; no time for you have I!

Hark! to the hazels Tityrus' summons rings!
—Alphesibœus to the mountain-ash—

Ad salices Aegon, ad flumina pulcher Amyntas,
Hîc gelidi fontes, hîc illita gramina musco,
Hîc Zephyri, hîc placidas interstrepit arbutus undas;
Ista canunt surdo, frutices ego nactus abibam.
    Ite domum impasti, domino jam non vacat, agni.

Mopsus ad hæc, nam me redeuntem fortè notarat
(Et callebat avium linguas, & sydera Mopsus)
Thyrsi quid hoc? dixit, quæ te coquit improba bilis?
Aut te perdit amor, aut te malè fascinat astrum
Saturni grave sæpe fuit pastoribus astrum,
Intimaque obliquo figit præcordia plumbo
    Ite domum impasti, domino jam non vacat, agni.

Mirantur nymphæ, & quid te Thyrsi futurum est?
Quid tibi vis? ajunt, non hæc solet esse juventæ
Nubila frons, oculique truces, vultusque severi

Ægon to the willows—to the river-plash
Comely Amyntas: 'Here (they call) are springs,
Cool springs, and mossy turf-enamellings!
Soft breathes the West! To gentle waters' flow
Arbutus interposeth whisperings low!'
I heed their pipings! The thickets gain'd, I go!
    Home, lambs, unfed; no time for you have I!

Here Mopsus, who had chanced my homing feet
To spy—he knew the speech of all that flies,
Mopsus, the star-gazer! 'What's this?' (he cries)
'Thyrsis, what froward spleen thy veins doth heat?
Art lost for love? o'erlookt by baleful star?
Oft Saturn has meant mischance where shepherds are—
Deep in their bosoms sinks his slanting lead!'
    Home, lambs, unfed; no time for you have I!

Marvelling, the nymphs 'What's coming to thee?' plead,
'Thyrsis, what lack'st? Is this youth's wonted gait—
Ire-darting eyes, crabb'd looks, and cloudy brows?

Illa choros, lususque leves, & semper amorem
Iure petit, bis ille miser qui serus amavit.
   Ite domum impasti, domino jam non vacat, agni.
Venit Hyas, Dryopéque, et filia Baucidis Aegle,
Docta modos, citharæque sciens, sed perdita fastu,
Venit Idumanii Chloris vicina fluenti,
Nil me blanditiæ, nil me solantia verba
Nil me, si quid adest, movet, aut spes ulla futuri.
   Ite domum impasti, domino jam non vacat, agni.
Hei mihi quam similes ludunt per prata juvenci
Omnes unanimi secum sibi lege sodales,
Nec magis hunc alio quisquam secernit amicum
De grege, sic densi veniunt ad pabula thoes,
Inque vicem hirsuti paribus junguntur onagri,
Lex eadem pelagi, deserto in littore Proteus

—Nay! dance and dalliance, love's unwearied vows
Are youth's! Twice luckless, who has lov'd o'erlate!'
   Home, lambs, unfed; no time for you have I!

   Came Hyas—Dryope—came (whom Baucis bore)
Mistress of measures, lutist, too, of skill,
   Aegle, whom pride doth kill!—
Came Chloris, she who dwelt by Chelmer's shore!—
Nought their kind words, soft speeches, solace me!
Nought recks me now that is, nor aught to be!
   Home, lambs, unfed; no time for you have I!

Alas, the well-matcht steers afield that sport,
All rul'd comrades by one impulse consort,
   Nor is from out the herd
   This friend to that preferr'd!—
So, in close pack, the jackals hunt their game;
Each hairy wild ass pairs, in turn, with each,
The law that rules in ocean is the same!
E'en Proteus, on his solitary beach,

Agmina Phocarum numerat, vilisque volucrum
Passer habet semper quicum sit, & omnia circum
Farra libens volitet serò sua tecta revisens,
Quem si fors letho objecit, seu milvus adunco
Fata tulit rostro, seu stravit arundine fossor,
Protinus ille alium socio petit inde volatu.
Nos durum genus, & diris exercita fatis
Gens, homines, aliena animis, & pectore discors
Vix sibi quisque parem de millibus invenit unum,
Aut si sors dederit tandem non aspera votis,
Illum inopina dies quâ non speraveris horâ
Surripit, æternum linquens in sæcula damnum.
    Ite domum impasti, domino jam non vacat, agni.

Counts o'er by companies his herded seals;
While, commonest of all the birds that fly,
    The sparrow constantly
Has other he may be with, when he wheels
At large o'er all the corn-fields, roosting late!
    Should fate that comrade smite
    By hooked beak of kite
    Or ditcher's reed prostrate,
With friendly swerve he seeks another mate!
We men, fate-harass'd, lead a sterner life;
Minds, all estrangement—hearts, that harbour strife!
    Scarce shalt thou find
E'en out of thousands, one true kindred mind!
Or if thy vows be not that bliss denied,
Some day, some hour unween'd of, shall betide
    To snatch him from thy side
Leaving thee agelong—nay, eternal loss!
    Home, lambs, unfed; no time for you have I!

Heu quis me ignotas traxit vagus error in oras
Ire per aereas rupes, Alpemque nivosam!
Ecquid erat tanti Romam vidisse sepultam?
Quamvis illa foret, qualem dum viseret olim,
Tityrus ipse suas & oves & rura reliquit;
Vt te tam dulci possem caruisse sodale
Possem tot maria alta, tot interponere montes,
Tot sylvas, tot saxa tibi, fluviosque sonantes.
Ah certè extremùm licuisset tangere dextram,
Et bene compositos placidè morientis ocellos,
Et dixisse vale, nostri memor ibis ad astra.
    Ite domum impasti, domino jam non vacat, agni.

Quanquam etiam vestri nunquam meminisse pigebit
Pastores Thusci, Musis operata juventus,

Alas, what gadding folly drew me aside
To visit shores I knew not of, and cross
Peaks hung aloft in heaven, and Alpine snow?—
Was there such need to see Rome's grave (e'en though
She were as Tityrus saw her, when he left
His flocks, his fields?)—and all to be bereft
Of thee, that wast so pleasant, Friend,—how dream
Twixt thee and me so many a deep to set—
Woods, rocks, nay many a range and roaring stream?
Ah, else I might thy dying eyelids yet
Have clos'd in peace, thine outreach'd hand have met,
    'Farewell' to say—
'Remember me upon thy starward way!'
    Home, lambs, unfed! no time for you have I!

Yet still, ye Tuscan shepherds, surely still
    I never can nor will
    At thoughts of you repine,
O youthful offerers at the Muses' shrine!

Hic Charis, atque Lepos; & Thuscus tu quoque Damon,*
Antiquâ genus unde petis Lucumonis ab urbe.
O ego quantus eram gelidi cum stratus ad Arni
Murmura, populeumque nemus, quà mollior herba,
Carpere nunc violas, nunc summas carpere myrtos
Et potui Lycidæ certantem audire Menalcam,
Ipse etiam tentare ausus sum, nec puto multùm
Displicui, nam sunt & apud me munera vestra
Fiscellæ, calathique, & cerea vincla cicutæ,
Quin & nostra suas docuerunt nomina fagos
Et Datis, & Francinus, erant & vocibus ambo
Et studiis noti, Lydorum sanguinis ambo.
    Ite domum impasti, domino iam non vacat, agni.

Hæc mihi tum læto dictabat roscida luna,
Dum solus teneros claudebam cratibus hædos.

* Ed. Pr. has
full-stop.

—Here 'Grace' and 'Charm' were, and (a Tuscan too),
Thou, Damon, thou whose house her founder drew
From that old city of the Lucumo!
    Oh, how transported was my mind, when I
Outstretch'd beside cool Arno's whispering flow,
In poplar glade, where tenderer grass doth grow,
Could violets pluck—or pluck the myrtles high,
And hear with Lycidas Menalcas vie!
I too dar'd sing nor greatly fail'd to please,
Methinks, since here—your gifts to me—are these
Winebowls, and waxbound pipes, and basketry!—
    Nay, even, rather, to his favourite beech
Either, of twain, to know my name did teach—
Dati—Francini, poet-scholars good,
Both famous, boasting both the Tuscan blood!
    Home, lambs, unfed; no time for you have I!

    These things, when I no grief did apprehend
The dewy moon kept crooning by and bye,
While lone, in wattled cotes, my kids I penn'd.

15

Ah quoties dixi, cùm te cinis ater habebat,
Nunc canit, aut lepori nunc tendit retia Damon,
Vimina nunc texit, varios sibi quod sit in usus;
Et quæ tum facili sperabam mente futura
Arripui voto levis, et præsentia finxi,
Heus bone numquid agis? nisi te quid fortè retardat
Imus? et argutâ paulùm recubamus in umbra,
Aut ad aquas Colni, aut ubi jugera Cassibelauni?
Tu mihi percurres medicos, tua gramina, succos,
Helleborúmque, humilésque crocos, foliúmque* hyacinthi,
Quasque habet ista palus herbas, artesque medentum
(Ah pereant herbæ, pereant artesque medentum
Gramina, postquam ipsi nil profecere magistro.)
Ipse etiam, nam nescio quid mihi grande sonabat

* Ed. Pr.
foliumq;
hyacinthi.

How oft, when blacken'd ash held all my friend,
Unto myself I said: 'Now Damon sings,
Now haply for a hare his nets he flings,
Now weaves him osiers for their several use!'
Thus all I did, so sure, of future muse,
  My winged wishes came
To seize and as of present time, did frame!
—'Hail, friend, what's doing? If by nought you're stay'd
Shall we be off, and for a while be laid
To rest, recline 'neath the clear-singing shade
By Colne waters, or lands of Cassivellaun?
Thou shalt recount me virtuous juices drawn
From thy choice simples—low-growing saffron, or
Foliage of hyacinth and hellebore;—
And herbs whereof that fen of thine hath store,
  And Med'cine's "arts that heal!"'—
Oh, wither the "herbs"!—oh, wither "arts that heal"
And simples, that could not work their master's weal!
  I, for my part—twas hence the 'leven-night,
And one more day—my oat some loftier flight

Fistula, ab undecimâ iam lux est altera nocte,
Et tum forte novis admôram labra cicutis,
Dissiluere tamen ruptâ compage, nec ultra
Ferre graves potuere sonos, dubito quoque ne sim
Turgidulus, tamen et referam, vos cedite, silvæ
    Ite domum impasti, domino iam non vacat, agni

Ipse ego Dardanias Rutupina per ęquora puppes
Dicam, & Pandrasidos regnum vetus Inogeniæ
Brennúmque Arviragúmque duces, priscúmque Belinum
Et tandem Armoricos Britonum sub lege colonos;
Tum gravidam Arturo fatali fraude Iogernen
Mendaces vultus, assumptáque Gorlois arma
Merlini dolus. O mihi tum si vita supersit,
Tu procul annosa pendebis fistula pinu
Multùm oblita mihi, aut patriis mutata camænis

Of song essaying—had just applied my lip
To those new reeds, when they apart did slip,
Snapping their band, whereafter they no more
    Their loftier tones could pour!
E'en now, misgives me lest I may
    Pretentious make my lay—
Nay, I will tell it! Silvan songs, give way!
    Home, lambs, unfed! no time for you have I!

Of Trojan ships that rode off Richboro's strand
I'll sing, and of the ancient royal land
Of Inogen, daughter of King Pandrasus—
Of Belin olden, Dukes Bran, Arviragus,—
Then, Armoric settlers rul'd from Britain's Isle—
Next, of Igraine, that was, by fatal wile,
Of Arthur's birth expectant, through the guile
Of lying looks, and arms of Gorlois ta'en,
Merlin's untruth!—Oh last, should life remain,
On yon old pine, my pipes, you'll hang again,
Forgot, how much! or for your native Muse

Brittonicum strides, quid enim? omnia non licet uni
Non sperasse uni licet omnia, mi satis ampla
Merces, & mihi grande decus (sim ignotus in ævum
Tum licet, externo penitúsque inglorius orbi)
Si me flava comas legat Vsa, & potor Alauni,
Vorticibúsque frequens Abra, & nemus omne Treantæ,
Et Thamesis meus ante omnes, & fusca metallis
Tamara, & extremis me discant Orcades undis
    Ite domum impasti, domino iam non vacat, agni.

Hęc tibi servabam lentâ sub cortice lauri
Hæc, & plura simul, tum quæ mihi pocula Mansus
Mansus, Chalcidicæ non ultima gloria ripæ,
Bina dedit mirum artis opus, mirandus & ipse,
Et circum gemino cælaverat argumento:
In medio rubri maris unda, & odoriferum ver

The shrilling sound of Britain's war-pipe chuse!
But what? O'ermuch for one all things to be,
Or all to have hop'd—guerdon enough for me,
Fame great enough—(for aye unknown I'd bide,
Inglorious quite to all the world beside)
So fairhair'd Ouse, and they who Allen drink,
Much swirling Severn*, and all Trent's bowery brink,
—Thou, chief, my Thames—and Tamar swart with ore,
And utmost Orkney's waves, shall con me o'er!
    Home, lambs, unfed! no time for you have I !

* or, Humber.

These, in tough baybark wrapt, I kept for thee,
—More, the twin cups that Manso gave to me—
    (Manso, whose fame shall be
Not the least glory of old Naples' shore),
Each wondrous—like their master—who had wrought
Them round about with train of linked thought,
Graven on either side in answering moods,
The Red Sea middest, and odour-breathing spring;

18

Littora longa Arabum, & sudantes balsama silvæ
Has inter Phœnix divina avis, unica terris
Cæruleum fulgens diversicoloribus alis
Auroram vitreis surgentem respicit undis.
Parte alia Polus omnipatens, & magnus Olympus,
Quis putet? hic quoque Amor pictæque in nube pharetræ
Arma corusca faces, & spicula tincta pyropo
Nec tenues animas, pectúsque ignobile vulgi
Hinc ferit, at circùm flammantia lumina torquens
Semper in erectum spargit sua tela per orbes
Impiger, & pronos nunquam collimat ad ictus,
Hinc mentes ardere sacræ, formeque deorum.
   Tu quoque in his, nec me fallit spes lubrica Damon,
Tu quoque in his certè es, nam quò tua dulcis abiret
Sanctáque simplicitas, nam quò tua candida virtus?

With those far coasts of Araby, and woods
  A-sweat with tears of balm,
Where Phoenix, bird divine, with iris'd wing,
(Sole-born on earth), an azurn flame doth fling;
While to her back regard doth ocean's calm
The mirror'd image of the Dawnrise bring!
Then great Olympus, on the reverse hand,
And—breadth illimitable—the heav'ns expand!
What, are Love's quivers, cloud-painted, here on high?
—Brands, glittering bow, darts dipt in gold-bronze dye?—
He wounds not hence slight souls, the common cry,
But throwing far abroad his blazing eyne,
Strews through the spheres his darts, in upward line
Tireless, and aimeth ne'er a lowlier blow;
Hence, sacred minds and godlike shapes do glow!
Thou among these—(for sure no smooth surmise
Deludes me, Damon!) now most surely art!
For whither else should wend thy single heart
So heavenly mild—thy virtues' shining guise?

Nec te Lethæo fas quæsivisse sub orco,
Nec tibi conveniunt lachrymae, nec flebimus ultrà,
Ite procul lachrymæ, purum colit ęthera Damon,
Aethera purus habet, pluvium pede reppulit arcum
Heroúmque animas inter, divósque perennes
Aethereos haurit latices & gaudia potat
Ore Sacro. Quin tu cœli post jura recepta
Dexter ades, placidúsque fave quicúnque vocaris,
Seu tu noster eris Damon, sive ęquior audis

* Ed. Pr.
Diodotus

Diodatus*, quo te divino nomine cuncti
Cęlicolæ nôrint, sylvísque vocabere Damon.
Quod tibi purpureus pudor, & sine labe juventus
Grata fuit, quòd nulla tori libata voluptas,
En etiam tibi virginei servantur honores,

How wrong to have sought in that forgetful Deep
Thee whom no tears befit!—No more I'll weep!
Begone, my tears! He dwells in those pure skies,
Himself all pure! And doth our rainbow spurn,
Where mid heroic souls and gods eterne,
Celestial streams and pleasures slake the drouth
    Of his new-purged mouth!
Do thou, when heard thou hast heavn's each decree,
With lucky words, calm presence, favour me,
What name soever thou wouldst rather hear,
Our Damon, or that sacred name that's dear
To all the saints, Diodati? What though!
Thou'lt still be Damon to our woods below!
Since thy bright honour and thy youth unstain'd
    Have equal favour gain'd,
    Since to no earthly lust
    Thou didst thy body trust,
Behold the honours of virginity
    Laid up for thee on high,

Ipse caput nitidum cinctus rutilante corona,
Lętáque frondentis gestans umbracula* palmæ,
Aeternùm perages immortales hymenęos
Cantus ubi, choreisque furit lyra mista beatis
Festa Sionęo bacchantur & Orgia Thyrso.

*Ed. Pr.
umbtacula

FINIS.   Londini

Where thou, thy bright brow ring'd with flashing gold,
Broad umbrage of triumphal palm shalt hold,
  And evermore as guest
Of the unexpressive marriage-feast partake
Where dance and song tempestuous concent make
  With harpings of the blest,
And Sion's 'Rod' His mysticks doth unite
In one high phrensy of the ecstatick Rite!

For EU product safety concerns, contact us at Calle de José Abascal, 56–1°,
28003 Madrid, Spain or eugpsr@cambridge.org.

www.ingramcontent.com/pod-product-compliance
Ingram Content Group UK Ltd.
Pitfield, Milton Keynes, MK11 3LW, UK
UKHW030902150625
459647UK00021B/2653